AF270626

Vizslas

by Julie Murray

Abdo Kids Jumbo is an Imprint of Abdo Kids
abdobooks.com

abdobooks.com

Published by Abdo Kids, a division of ABDO, P.O. Box 398166, Minneapolis, Minnesota 55439.
Copyright © 2024 by Abdo Consulting Group, Inc. International copyrights reserved in all countries.
No part of this book may be reproduced in any form without written permission from the publisher.
Abdo Kids Jumbo™ is a trademark and logo of Abdo Kids.

Printed in the United States of America, North Mankato, Minnesota.

102023

012024

THIS BOOK CONTAINS
RECYCLED MATERIALS

Photo Credits: Getty Images, Shutterstock, Thinkstock

Production Contributors: Teddy Borth, Jennie Forsberg, Grace Hansen
Design Contributors: Candice Keimig, Pakou Moua

Library of Congress Control Number: 2023937690
Publisher's Cataloging-in-Publication Data

Names: Murray, Julie, author.

Title: Vizslas / by Julie Murray

Description: Minneapolis, Minnesota : Abdo Kids, 2024 | Series: Dogs | Includes online resources and index.

Identifiers: ISBN 9781098268541 (lib. bdg.) | ISBN 9781098269241 (ebook) | ISBN 9781098269593 (Read-to-Me ebook)

Subjects: LCSH: Vizsla--Juvenile literature. | Hungarian pointer--Juvenile literature. | Dogs--Juvenile literature. | Dogs--Behavior--Juvenile literature. | Animal behavior--Juvenile literature.

Classification: DDC 599.772--dc23

Table of Contents

Vizslas

Vizslas can be traced back more than 1,000 years to Hungary. They were **bred** to hunt with great speed and ease.

Europe
Hungary
Africa
N
E
S
W

Vizslas are medium-sized dogs.

They are sleek and muscular.

They stand 24 inches (61 cm) tall

and weigh 65 pounds (29.5 kg).

Their bodies are made to move!

The Vizsla has a short, smooth coat. It is golden-rust in color. The dog has a long, square-shaped **muzzle** and long ears. It holds its tail even with its body.

Vizslas love to be active outdoors. However, they do not have an **undercoat**. They get cold easily. A jacket can help in cold and rainy weather.

Grooming

Vizslas require little grooming. Brushing with a soft, rubber brush once a week will keep their coats shiny. Their nails should be trimmed every few weeks.

Exercise

Vizslas have endless energy. They need daily exercise and a large area to run and play. They enjoy running alongside their owners.

Vizslas love to keep busy.
They enjoy field work and
training exercises. They also do
well in **agility training**!

Personality

Vizslas make good family dogs, but they need proper training and exercise. They are best for active owners.

Vizslas are smart, **loyal**, and loving. They want to be near their owners. Being alone for too long will make them sad. They do best with lots of love and attention.

More Facts

- Vizslas are fast. They can run up to 40 miles per hour (64.4 kph)!

- They are excellent swimmers and love the water. However, they are unable to stay in the water too long, because they will get cold.

- Vizslas were recognized by the American Kennel Club in 1960. They are members of the Sporting Group.

Glossary

agility training – a type of exercise training that incorporates short bursts of movement that involve changes of direction.

bred – developed over time for a certain purpose.

loyal – showing devotion and faithfulness to someone.

muzzle – the part of the head of some animals that contains the nose, jaws, and mouth.

undercoat – the short hairs growing close to an animal's skin, covered by longer hair or fur.

Index

Abdo Kids ONLINE
FREE! ONLINE MULTIMEDIA RESOURCES

Visit **abdokids.com** to access crafts, games, videos, and more!